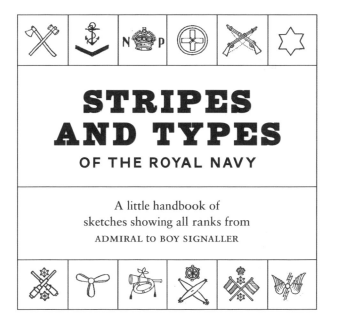

STRIPES AND TYPES

OF THE ROYAL NAVY

A little handbook of
sketches showing all ranks from
ADMIRAL to BOY SIGNALLER

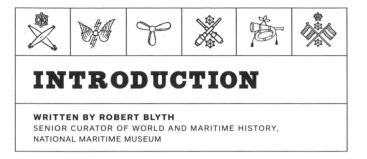

INTRODUCTION

WRITTEN BY ROBERT BLYTH
SENIOR CURATOR OF WORLD AND MARITIME HISTORY,
NATIONAL MARITIME MUSEUM

STRIPES AND TYPES OF THE ROYAL NAVY
is a light-hearted, but fairly thorough, examination of
the hierarchical structure – and the associated roles,
responsibilities and uniforms – of the Edwardian
Royal Navy. In total, 27 different ranks or positions
are illustrated, but even this apparent complexity
masks the convoluted reality of the early-twentieth-
century navy. In the age of sail, there were certain
'specialisms' – boatswain, carpenter, sailing master,
surgeon, etc. – but seamen and officers were, for the
most part, jacks of all trades. Technological change in
the nineteenth century spelt the end of the so-called
'handyman Tar' as new equipment and methods of
propulsion led to the rise of more 'expert' servicemen,
focusing on areas like engineering, gunnery,

navigation, signals and torpedoes. Each new technical development – radio, submarines, naval air power – required new and greater specialisation, which was reflected in the uniforms and badges that signified rank and role.

In *Stripes and Types* each rank is shown wearing a distinctive uniform and, in some cases, a particular 'dress' is indicated: working rig, mess undress, full dress, etc. What officers and men wore not only depended on their rank and in which branch of the Royal Navy they served, but also on where they were (at sea, ashore, in the tropics or more temperate climes) and whether the occasion was formal or workaday. For officers, there were at least ten different 'dresses', or styles of uniform, to cover the range of different circumstances they might encounter in the course of their naval duties, from warfare or waltzing to the icy chill of Arctic waters and the searing heat of the Persian Gulf.

As the 'Senior Service', the Royal Navy had a degree of prestige and eminence attached to it which was certainly reflected in officers' uniforms. Since the first introduction of uniforms in 1748, these broadly reflected the changes in men's civilian fashions. Those shown in *Stripes and Types* are of the 1901 pattern which was gradually adjusted over time – with regulations making changes to the numbers of

ADMIRAL SIR JOHN FISHER IS WEARING ADMIRAL'S
BALL DRESS, REFLECTING NOT ONLY THE RANGE OF
OFFICERS' UNIFORMS, BUT ALSO HIS KEEN INTEREST
IN BALLROOM DANCING.

buttons, widths of braiding, etc. – before being more comprehensively altered when a new pattern was introduced in 1924. As a result, the officers of the Royal Navy certainly kept British tailors busy.

In contrast, the uniforms of ratings, or ordinary seamen, were far removed from the general development of fashion. Most men in the navy wore a form of 'square rig', a simple outfit consisting of bell-bottomed trousers and a shirt or jersey top with a wide, blue-trimmed collar, which harked back to the stout-hearted, loyal Jack Tars (seamen) of the days of sail. Of course, all of the individuals depicted are men. There were no women in naval uniform until the creation of the Women's Royal Naval Service in 1917 and none saw active service at sea in warships until as late as 1990.

When *Stripes and Types* was first published in 1909, the Royal Navy was the biggest and most technologically advanced fleet in the world. A large navy was needed not only to defend the British Isles but also to safeguard Britain's position as a global power. The territories of the vast and growing British Empire spanned every continent. Britain's trading and commercial interests stretched even further afield. Crucially, the nation relied on the import of food to feed the British populations and a steady stream of raw materials to supply the nation's mills, factories

and furnaces. Britain's wealth was generated by
the export of goods. All of these vital imports and
exports were carried by sea. Moreover, the activities of
Britain's huge merchant fleet meant that British ships
carried much of the world's international trade too.
This sprawling imperial and trading system required
Royal Navy vessels to be stationed across the globe,
patrolling all the major seas and oceans to ensure sea
lanes were secure and that goods flowed freely.

THIS ATMOSPHERIC
PAINTING SHOWS
THE BRITISH
DREADNOUGHT FLEET
ARRIVING AT SPITHEAD
FOR GEORGE V'S
CORONATION REVIEW
IN JUNE 1911.

The Royal Navy had enjoyed superiority at sea since
the end of the Napoleonic Wars (1793–1815) but, by
1909, foreign powers were challenging Britain's naval
dominance. The Royal Navy tried to maintain a 'two-
power standard' requiring the British fleet to be larger
than the combined strength of its two greatest rivals.
At the beginning of the twentieth century, Germany
started a major programme of naval expansion with
the express aim of undermining the Royal Navy's

HMS *DREADNOUGHT* WAS BUILT SWIFTLY AND
IN GREAT SECRECY AT PORTSMOUTH BEFORE
ITS LAUNCH ON 10 FEBRUARY 1906.

pre-eminence. Britain's response to the Kaiser's
ambitions was a daring advance in battleship
technology that tore up the naval rule book.
This technological leap took the form of HMS
Dreadnought, an all-big-gun battleship launched
in 1906, which made every other warship obsolete,
including, of course, those of the Royal Navy.

Ship construction programmes halted as nations
reacted to this naval revolution. Dreadnoughts were
very expensive to build and only a handful of powers,
including Germany, attempted to join Britain in
what became a naval arms race in the years before

the First World War. Ultimately, the British won this competition by being able to out-build Germany. But when *Stripes and Types* was produced, this Anglo-German rivalry was at its height and was regarded by many as a race for national survival. This book's light tone, therefore, masks the seriousness of the situation, but its aim – to 'interest and educate the public mind in the men who constitute the first line of our defensive forces' – reflected Britain's naval pre-occupation at the time. Indeed, it had barely been on sale for a year when the Royal Navy launched HMS *Orion*, the first 'super-dreadnought', making battleships even more powerful. With a wartime crew of over 1,100 men, this mighty warship would have accommodated almost all of the 'stripes and types' illustrated in this reprint of the 1909 original, from admiral to boy signaller.

STRIPES AND TYPES

OF THE

ROYAL NAVY

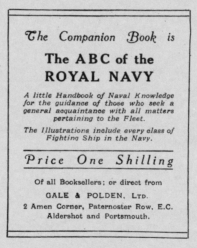

STRIPES AND TYPES

OF THE

ROYAL NAVY

A LITTLE HANDBOOK OF SKETCHES BY NAVAL OFFICERS
SHOWING THE DRESS AND DUTIES OF ALL
RANKS FROM ADMIRAL TO
BOY SIGNALLER

BY

F.W.R.M. AND J.S.H.

LONDON:
GALE & POLDEN, LTD.,
2 AMEN CORNER, PATERNOSTER ROW, E.C.
WELLINGTON WORKS, ALDERSHOT,
and
NELSON WORKS, PORTSMOUTH.

London :

GALE & POLDEN, Ltd.,

2 Amen Corner, Paternoster Row, E.C.

—

1909

STRIPES AND TYPES

◎

Admiral. · *Vice-Admiral.* · *Rear-Admiral*

Publishers' Note

Notwithstanding the vital importance of the British Fleet, very little is known of the men upon whom the responsibility for its efficiency falls, and *Stripes and Types* has been prepared so that the Dress and Duties of Officers and Men of the Royal Navy may become better known to the British People.

With the increasing attention now given to the Fleet it is hoped that this little book will meet with a reception similar to that given to the *A B C of the Royal Navy*, and will interest and educate the public mind in the men who constitute the first line of our defensive forces.

Gale & Polden Ltd

DISTINCTIVE RANKS of OFFICERS in the ROYAL NAVY

CIVIL BRANCH

EXECUTIVE BRANCH

ENGINEER	MEDICAL	ACCOUNTANT	CARPENTERS

Admiral of the Fleet — Lieutenant over 8 years Seniority — Engineer Vice Admiral — Chief Artificer Engineer — Inspector General of Hospitals & Fleets — Paymaster in Chief — Carpenter Lieutenant

Admiral — Lieutenant under 8 years Seniority — Engineer Rear Admiral — Artificer Engineer over 10 years Seniority — Deputy Inspector General of Hospitals & Fleets — Fleet Paymaster — Chief Carpenter

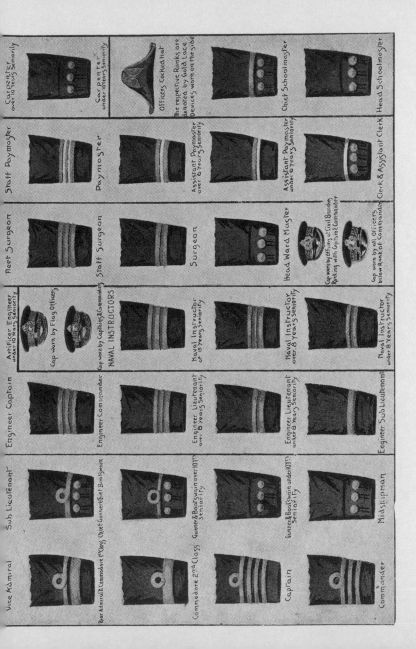

Vice Admiral

Sub Lieutenant

Engineer Captain

Artificer Engineer
under 10 Years Seniority

Fleet Surgeon

Staff Paymaster

Carpenter
over 10 Years Seniority

Rear Admiral & Commodore 1st Class | Chief Gunner & Chief Boatswain

Engineer Commander

Cap worn by Flag Officers

Cap worn by Captains & Commanders
NAVAL INSTRUCTORS

Staff Surgeon

Paymaster

Officers Cocked Hat
The respective Ranks are
denoted by Gold Lace
Devices worn on the side

Commodore 2nd Class

Gunner & Boatswain over 10 Years Seniority

Engineer Lieutenant
over 8 Years Seniority

Naval Instructor
of 15 Years Seniority

Surgeon

Assistant Paymaster
over 6 Years Seniority

Chief Schoolmaster

Gunner & Boatswain under 10 Years Seniority

Engineer Lieutenant
under 8 Years Seniority

Naval Instructor
over 8 Years Seniority

Head Ward Master

Cap worn by Officers of Civil Branches
Ranking with Captain & Commander

Assistant Paymaster
under 6 Years Seniority

Head Schoolmaster

Commander

Captain

Midshipman

Engineer Sub Lieutenant

Naval Instructor
under 8 Years Seniority

Cap worn by all Officers
below Rank of Commander

Clerk & Assistant Clerk

DISTINGUISHING BADGES of PETTY OFFICERS, MEN AND BOYS IN THE ROYAL NAVY.

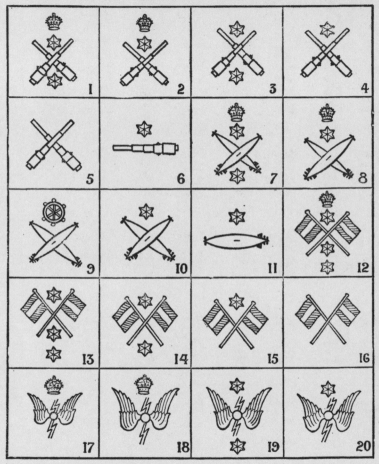

(1) Gunner's Mate and Gunlayer, 1st Class. (2) Gunner's Mate. (3) Gunlayer, 1st Class. (4) Gunlayer, 2nd Class. (5) Gunlayer, 3rd Class. (6) Seaman Gunner and P.O. (G) (Not Gunlayer or Gunner's Mate). (7) Torpedo Gunner's Mate, Higher Standard. (8) Torpedo Gunner's Mate. (9) Torpedo Coxswain. (10) Leading Torpedo Man. (11) Seaman Torpedo Man and P.O. (T). (12) Chief Yeoman of Signals. (13) Yeoman of Signals. (14) Leading Signalman. (15) Signalman. (16) Ordinary Signalman and Signal Boy. (17) Chief Petty Officer Telegraphist. (18) Petty Officer Telegraphist. (19) Leading Telegraphist. (20) Telegraphist.

DISTINGUISHING BADGES of PETTY OFFICERS, MEN AND BOYS IN THE ROYAL NAVY

(21) Ordinary and Boy Telegraphist. (22) Good Shooting Badge, 1st Class. (23) Good Shooting Badge, 2nd Class. (24) Good Shooting Badge, 3rd Class. (25) Physical Training Instructor, 1st Class. (26) Physical Training Instructor, 2nd Class. (27) Mechanician. (28) Chief Stoker. (29) All other Stokers. (30) Chief and other Armourers. (31) Armourers' Mates and Crews. (32) Blacksmith, Plumber, Painter, 1st Class. All Chief and other Carpenter's Mates, and skilled Shipwrights of whatever rating. (33) All other Artificers. (34) Naval Police. (35) Gold Star :—Schoolmaster, Ship's Steward, Ships Steward's Assistant. Ships Steward's Boy, all Writers ; Silver Star : Cook. (36) Sick Berth Staff. (37) Buglers.

BADGES OF RATING AND GOOD CONDUCT BADGES.

(38) Leading Seamen, Leading Signalmen, Shipwrights, Leading Carpenter's Crew, and Ships Steward's Assistants over three years service. (39) Second Class Petty Officer. This rating is dying out. (40) First Class Petty Officer.

THE ADMIRAL.

There are four different kinds of Admirals :—
" Admiral of the Fleet," " Admiral," " Vice-Admiral,"
and " Rear Admiral." Admirals of the Fleet are not
employed afloat : the other three are given commands
of Fleets, Admirals having the largest number of ships
under their control, Vice-Admirals a lesser number,
whereas a mere Rear-Admiral boasts of but a few
ships in which he can enforce his orders. A very
large amount of responsibility rests with an Admiral,
especially in time of war. He it is who finds the
enemy, and, having arranged his Fleet to the best
advantage, defeats him with the loss of as few ships as
possible. In peace time he orders all kinds of Evolutions
and General Drills to be performed in the Fleet ; he
takes his ships to sea and exercises them in various for-
mations, and is responsible to the Lords Commissioners
of the Admiralty that his entire command is O.K.

THE VICE-ADMIRAL
(Working Dress).

THE FLAG CAPTAIN.

The "Flag Captain" differs from the ordinary "common or garden" Captain, in that he is borne in a ship which carries an Admiral—hence the term "Flag," for Admirals on the "Active List" always fly their particular flag.

The "Flag Captain," like other Captains, is in supreme command of his ship. At sea he is generally on the Bridge, supervising the navigation and conning of the ship. In harbour he supervises the General Drills, whacks out punishment of the more serious nature—where punishment is needed—and, besides being the ultimate "Court of Appeal" in ALL matters on board, is responsible to his Admiral for anything and everything which is done amiss, or which is NOT done, by any single individual on board. Happy the Captain who is well served by his Officers—and, thank goodness, they nearly all are.

THE FLAG CAPTAIN.

THE ADMIRAL'S SECRETARY

is a Fleet- or Staff-Paymaster or Paymaster, detached for special duty with the Admiral, whose right-hand man he is, with regard to business matters. Daily he waits upon him, answers his correspondence as directed, keeps him fully informed as to the "King's Regulations" upon the hundred-and-one things which crop up every minute ; follows him when he "inspects" ships, and sees that all the books kept by the Officers in the "inspected" ship, are correct. The Secretary has his meals with the Admiral, takes him for exercise ashore, when the ship is in harbour, and is absolutely invaluable as guide, philosopher, and friend. A good Secretary will see a bad Admiral through his duties all right (should one ever be able to find a bad Admiral !), but a bad Secretary would jeopardise the best Admiral who ever stepped into a pair of top boots.

SECRETARY
(Mess Undress).

THE FLAG LIEUTENANT

is employed entirely by the Admiral. He is a "Signal" specialist, having gone through a course of "Morse," "Semaphore," etc., to fit him for supervising the signals which are sent by the Admiral to his Captains in other ships. He attends on the Admiral at all times, has his meals with him, helps him to entertain his guests, and goes ashore with him, as well as being his right-hand man when "Inspections" of ships are in progress, etc. At sea, he is constantly on the Bridge with the Admiral, helping him in every way. Besides these and numerous other duties, he lectures to the Midshipmen upon the various branches of signalling ; so that, altogether, a Flag Lieutenant must be very much "all there" in order to fulfil his duties, and give satisfaction to his Admiral.

THE FLAG LIEUTENANT
(Full Dress).

THE COMMANDER.

The Commander, who ranks next to the Captain, is perhaps the busiest man on board. His duties are multitudinous—from early morn to dewy eve he is "at it." He runs the whole routine of the ship, and tells off all the "Hands" for their special stations which they have to take up at different times. For instance, men are stationed at different parts of the ship for evolutions—"Out" and "In" Torpedo Nets, Ships taken in tow, Fire Stations, Collision Stations, General Quarters (when everyone is ready for a fight), etc., etc. Besides all this, he sees a huge mass of signals which come to the ship about all sorts and conditions of things, whacks out all punishments, save for the more serious crimes, which he passes on to the Captain, and is constantly roaming about the ship to see that it is kept clean. These are merely a few of his arduous duties, but space prevents . . .

THE COMMANDER.

THE FIRST LIEUTENANT

(or " No. 1 " as he is usually called), is another busy man on board. Very often he is either a " Navigating," " Gunnery," or "Torpedo" Specialist. If the first, he is responsible, under the Captain, for the safe navigation of the ship. He sets all the courses, obtains the position of the ship from time to time throughout the day, keeps his Chronometers wound and knows all their errors on Greenwich Mean Time, and pilots the ship safely back into harbour again. He also has charge of all the charts which are constantly having to be corrected as fresh information comes in. If he is a " Gunnery" Specialist, he has the entire charge of all the firing in the ship. He sees that the guns are kept in good condition, that the ammunition is always at the proper temperature, and that the thousand-and-one things connected with gunnery are in proper order. If he is a " Torpedo" Specialist, besides supervising all the torpedoes in the ship, seeing they are kept clean and ready for action, and, when occasion arises, firing them, he has the entire charge of the Electric Lighting and the Wireless Telegraphy Department. This latter, of course, is most important in the Navy, at the present time. The First Lieutenant is always in charge of some large part of the ship, of which he is responsible for the cleanliness. Should he happen not to be one of the above " Specialists," he takes some of the lesser duties of the over-worked Commander on his shoulders.

FIRST LIEUTENANT

A "WATCH-KEEPING LIEUTENANT,"

whilst on "Watch," is, under the Captain, in charge of the ship. If in harbour, he paces the Quarter-deck, sees to the "running" of all the boats, inspects every man who disembarks and comes on board, and is, generally speaking, responsible, at the time, for the safety of the ship. Besides all this, any complaints are brought before him. If at sea, he is again in charge of the ship when on "Watch," of course, under the Captain. He lives on the "Fore Bridge," and sees that the Quartermaster is steering the proper course as set by the Navigator. He takes observations and checks the ship's position from time to time, and is responsible for the entire safety of the ship. When not on "Watch," he has all sorts of duties. A certain number of men are specially under him, and he sees that they are present at "Divisions," that they have the proper amount of clothes, and that everything connected with his particular company of men, is correct.

THE LIEUTENANT.

THE ENGINEER COMMANDER

is the supreme head on board, of all the Engineering Department. Under him are, perhaps, three Engineering Lieutenants, Artificer Engineers, Engine-room Artificers, Mechanician, Chief Stoker, Stokers, etc. He is responsible to the Captain that all goes well. This means a great deal; for Battleships now have about 20 or more boilers (some ships have as many as 48), and, besides the main, there are dozens of Auxiliary Engines, such as those that work the Capstans, the Winches, the Steam-steering gear, the Refrigerating Machinery (to keep the Magazines cool), the Dynamos, etc., etc. All these engines require constant attention, and, should the least thing go wrong—well—the Engineer Commander has to suffer ! ! ! Besides the engines, he is responsible, with the Carpenter, for the hull of the ship; and he has to make returns periodically of all the Engine-room stores expended, the amount of coal used, how much of the latter there is on board, etc., etc. Surely the responsibility of the Engineer Commander is all but limitless ! !

ENGINEER COMMANDER.

THE ENGINEER LIEUTENANT.

A Battleship carries perhaps three Engineer Lieutenants. The "Senior" of these is often the hardest worked man in the ship. His duties are never-ending. The whole of the work of the Engine-room Department goes through him, for he is the "Organiser." He sees that all the orders of the Engineer Commander are carried out, tells off the many hands under him for their "stations," and allots all the work. He orders the number of boilers to be kept with steam, supervising personally everything that goes on. There is always work, for the bearings of every one of the engines on board are constantly wearing down, some have to be renewed, others filed down, and every one of them has constantly to be kept in adjustment. If he is not the "Senior," he keeps "Watch" down in the engine-room, and is responsible, at the time, for everything which may happen down there, expected or unexpected—and the unexpected often happens ! ! All complaints are brought before him. When not on "Watch," he has his "Division" of Stokers to look after, seeing that they have their proper amount of kit from time to time. Besides this, he takes one department of the Engine-room under his special supervision.

ENGINEER LIEUTENANT
(Working Rig).

THE MAJOR, ROYAL MARINE ARTILLERY,

who is only borne in a Flagship, is in command of all- the Marines on board, both Light Infantry and Artillery ; and is responsible to the Captain of the ship that all goes well. He sees that the proper drills are carried out, punishes his men (taking the more serious cases before the Commander for punishment), and sees that his Lieutenants R.M.A. and R.M.L.I. carry out their work. At times he lands with his own men, and Marines from other ships, taking charge of them all, and practising them in their drills.

He goes on board other ships, and inspects their Detachments, sending in his report to the Admiral. In his own ship he has a special "station" in action, possibly the "Main Top," where he controls the fire of a group of guns, or, should the Fore Top be disabled, he controls the fire of all the guns in the ship. The Major is not, as a rule, overworked, but he has a great deal of responsibility.

THE MAJOR,
Royal Marine Artillery
(*Working Dress*)

THE LIEUTENANT, ROYAL MARINE LIGHT INFANTRY,

has many and varied duties to perform. First of all, he is in command of his " Half Company," and has to see that all the men's clothes are clean, that they have a full kit, and that their arms are in good condition. He inspects them twice daily at " Divisions," and is usually in charge of the " Guard "—a body of Marines who are drawn up on the Quarter-deck, and salute when a Flagship is passing, or when a Vice- or Rear-Admiral is hovering about in the vicinity. He keeps "Watch" in harbour on the Quarter-deck like other Naval Officers, and, in action, is in charge of a group of guns.

Very often he is Assistant " Gunnery " or "Torpedo " Officer, with all the varied work which this entails. Thus, besides the duties of a soldier, he has to combine with them the qualifications of a Naval Officer, and also a " Specialist." Fortunate the Lieutenant R.M.L.I. who lived in days gone by, when things were less strenuous than they are now ! ! !

THE SUBALTERN,
Royal Marine Light Infantry
(Full Dress).

has a difficult task to fill on board. First of all, he has to " get on with " everyone, Officer and man, which means that he must not be in the least " straight-laced," but all the time he has to keep the " One Aim " constantly before him. On Sunday he has, perhaps, an Early Celebration, then at 10.30 comes Morning Service, which all those who are " Church of England " must attend. Then he has a Celebration after Service, and short Evening Service at about six o'clock. On week days he has Prayers at about 9.15, he regularly visits the " Sick Bay," talking to those who are ill ; at times he goes to the Cells, and sees the prisoners who have " broken their leave " or committed some other breach of Discipline. Every day he sets apart a portion of his time to " yarning " with the " Hands," and throughout the week has meetings for prayers, for the Members of the Naval Church Society, for those who belong to the Royal Naval Temperance Society, etc. He supervises the men's instruction as given by the Schoolmaster, and besides all these duties, he is constantly at work preparing his Sunday addresses. Very often he is a Naval Instructor as well ; in which case he instructs the Midshipmen in Applied Mechanics, Electricity, Navigation, etc., seeing that they take their Observations every day at sea, and work out the correct position of the ship. Perhaps an angel could satisfactorily fulfil a Chaplain's duties, nothing less—still, there are many very good substitutes.

THE CHAPLAIN.

THE FLEET SURGEON

has the entire charge of all the sick on board. Under him are one or two Surgeons, and perhaps three "Sick Berth Stewards" and "Attendants." Every day he reports to the Captain the number of men sick, and the nature of their illness. He attends the "Sick Bay" at certain hours, and, in conjunction with the Surgeon, inspects those who are unwell, ordering medicine or operating, as the case may be. At all times a Medical Officer is ready to attend to accidents, day and night. Cases which are too bad to be kept on board, the Fleet Surgeon sends to the nearest Naval Hospital. He makes arrangements for tending the wounded in battle, in some place free from shot and shell, and these arrangements are practised weekly at "General Quarters." Besides this, he is constantly reading the Medical Journals, and keeping himself acquainted with the latest advances of science. Truly is the "P.M.O." (Principal Medical Officer), as he is called, indispensable ! ! !

THE FLEET SURGEON

THE PAYMASTER

has charge of all the public monies in the ship, and of all "Slops," *i.e.*, materials for the men's clothing. The first of every month he pays both Officers and men. This is no light work, seeing that a Battleship's complement is anything between seven and nine hundred souls! Every book must be kept absolutely up-to-date, and every farthing accounted for. He is assisted by a staff of usually three or four—an Assistant Paymaster or Clerk, a "First Writer," a "Writer," and, perhaps, a "Boy Writer." He is responsible for the messing of the ship, and for this purpose has a staff of "Ship's Stewards" under him. This also entails a great amount of work. In addition to the above, he has his "station" in action—either "decoding" and "coding" wireless messages (for which he is temporarily in charge of the secret codes) or else assisting the Fleet Surgeon with the wounded, and rendering "First Aid." Who would be a Paymaster? Surely he earns the pay he gives himself ! ! !

STAFF PAYMASTER.

THE SUB-LIEUTENANT

ranks just below the Lieutenant. He is the head of the "Gun-room," where all Junior Officers and Midshipmen have their meals. Upon him lies the onerous task of seeing that the Midshipmen behave themselves, and that their conduct and language are as become "an Officer and a Gentleman." Should he fail in this—well —the Captain will have something to say to him! Like a Lieutenant, he has his "Division" of men to look after, and he keeps "Watch" in harbour. At sea he keeps "Watch" only under the supervision of a Lieutenant. Having passed out of the "Midshipman" stage, and reached the exalted rank of "Sub," he has to spend from nine to twenty-three months in this capacity, before their Lordships promote him, the length of time depending upon the number of marks obtained in his examination.

SUB-LIEUTENANT
(Frock Coat and Scales).

THE MIDSHIPMAN,

having spent four years ashore in a Naval Training Establishment, and put in six months at sea in a Cruiser, where he is supposed to learn the elements of his training as a Naval Officer, comes to sea in a Battleship or First-Class Cruiser at the age of about seventeen. Now begins his real training. He has one particular boat allotted to his entire charge, for which he is responsible ; and, whenever that boat leaves the ship, he goes too. He keeps his "Watch" in harbour and at sea, under the direct supervision of the "Officer of the Watch," from whom he learns all the various duties connected therewith, and he also has to assist a Lieutenant in looking after a "Division" of men. He is expected to keep his eyes "skinned," and learn how everything is carried out on board, and where all gear is stowed. Besides this, he has to attend lectures given by the "Navigating," "Gunnery," "Torpedo," and "Signal" Lieutenants. After six months of this training he will be employed for three months entirely in the Engine-room Department, under the Engineer Commander, until his three years' training is up, when he passes for "Sub-Lieutenant."

THE MIDSHIPMAN.

THE BOATSWAIN

(pronounced Bo'sun)

is a Warrant Officer, who looks after the general working of the ship, especially with regard to anchors, cables, blocks and tackles. He takes his orders from all Officers, more especially from the Commander. All ropes and hawsers are under his charge, and he is responsible that boats' "Falls," *i.e.*, the ropes used for hoisting and lowering boats, are renewed every six months, and changed end-for-end every three months. He is in charge of endless stores, such as rope, wire, wash-deck gear, and canvas, and he examines and passes men for higher "rating." Yes, he has quite enough to do, thank you ! ! !

The Gunner and the Carpenter are also Warrant Officers wearing the same dress.

THE BOATSWAIN.

CHIEF PETTY OFFICERS

embrace many different "ratings." There is the MASTER-AT-ARMS, who is the head of the Ship's Police; then there is the CHIEF GUNNERY INSTRUCTOR who sees to all the working of the guns, looks after the Magazines and Shell-rooms, and instructs the seamen in Gunnery. THE CHIEF QUARTERMASTER usually waits upon the Navigator, looks after the charts, etc., and, on the more important occasions, he steers the ship. THE CHIEF TORPEDO INSTRUCTOR sees to all the torpedoes, mining gear, electric lighting, dynamos, etc., and instructs those under him in the mysteries of his craft. THE CHIEF BO'SUN'S MATE "pipes," in a loud voice, throughout the ship, the orders given on deck for the different routine, and assists the Bo'sun generally. THE CHIEF PHYSICAL TRAINING INSTRUCTOR takes the Junior Officers and men in Physical drill. Besides these, there are Naval Schoolmasters, Chief Writers, Engine-room Artificers, Chief Armourers, Chief Cooks, Chief Bandmasters, Chief Stokers, Chief Sick-berth Stewards, etc., etc.

CHIEF PETTY OFFICER.

AN ENGINE-ROOM ARTIFICER

(or E.R.A. as he is usually called) is a very practical engineer. He repairs all sorts and kinds of defects, renews bearings of the engines, and, generally speaking, does all the engine-room metal-work in the ship. At sea he keeps "Watch" in the engine-room, and looks out for any and every order passed down from the Captain.

ENGINE-ROOM ARTIFICER.

THE PETTY OFFICER, FIRST-CLASS,

has charge of a body of men as Captain of a "part of the ship." If he is a QUARTERMASTER he sometimes pipes the orders for routine given on deck, instead of the Chief Bo'sun's Mate; he looks out for all boats coming alongside, and, at sea, he will, at times, steer the ship. If he is the COXSWAIN OF A BOAT, he steers his craft, takes charge of the hands in her, and generally sees her clean and efficient. The "P.O. 1" as he is called, embraces many different ratings :—Bo'sun's Mate, Gunnery Instructor, Torpedo Instructor, Physical Training Instructor, Ship's Corporal (*i.e.*, Police), 1st Writer, Yeoman of Signals, Sailmaker, Carpenter's Mate, Blacksmith, Armourer, Plumber, Painter ("Putty" he's always called), Cooper, Leading Stoker 1st Class, Sick-Berth Steward, Ship's Cook, Bandmaster, etc. All these names give one but a minute idea of the work which is done on board ship. Anyhow, these "P.O. Ones" are a fine body of men.

First-Class Petty Officer,
Yeoman of Signals
(Half Whites).

THE WRITER.

Just a line as to the FIRST WRITER'S duties :—
He is at his books all day long. He keeps the ship's
ledgers, makes out all kinds of " returns," " tots up "
the monies paid to the men and generally assists the
Paymaster. Very often he is Schoolmaster and
Librarian as well !

FIRST WRITER.

have no pleasant job. They maintain discipline in general, constantly patrolling the ship to see that everything is O.K. Having investigated an irregularity, they bring the culprit before the Commander for judgment, and keep a record of all punishments, as well as checking the wines and spirits coming into the ship. They take charge of all prisoners in cells or awaiting punishment, of all men's effects who are in hospital, sick, on long leave, or in prison ; they attend the " issue " of all spirits, " slops," clothing, money, and 'baccy, and see that no unwholesome food comes into the ship. Letters and parcels are delivered and despatched by them, and they look after the Midshipmen's hammocks, seeing them up and down at the proper time. Besides all these duties, they have the supervision of the men's messes, and are responsible that the proper hands go away in their boats, and attend their " Gun's Crews," etc. The Police have a difficult number to fill, being always connected with punishments, which is naturally disliked ; still, their unpleasant duties are ably done, and many of them are most popular in spite of everything.

SHIP'S CORPORAL
(No. 2's).

"ABLE-BODIED" AND "ORDINARY" SEAMEN

(*i.e.*, A.B's and O.S's) have much the same duties differing in the fact that the former have passed an examination, and are of higher rank than the latter. They do the manual work of the ship, such as cleaning and scrubbing. They help hoist the boats, splice ropes and wires, take their hand at an oar, and, at sea, steer the ship (an "A.B." does this), heave the lead, etc. Besides this, they "coal ship," and splash Admiralty grey paint about to make her look nice. They do all sorts of drills and evolutions, and, once a week in harbour, they land and carry out a march, perhaps scaling and taking some well-nigh impregnable fortress ! Then they also form part of a gun's crew, where they hoist ammunition up, load the gun, sponge her out, etc. At the present day, an "A.B." has to be pretty smart if he is going to get on.

ABLE SEAMAN
(Marching Order).

THE STOKER'S

job is not all beer and skittles, and there is any amount of work going on at all times. At sea a "Watch" must be kept in the Engine-room or Stoke-hole. In the latter case, coal has constantly to be shovelled to keep the fires going. Then again, other Stokers are employed in "trimming" coal, and fetching it from the "bunkers" to the boilers. Generally speaking, the Stokers do all the manual work of the Engineering Department. In harbour there are always fire-grates to be scraped out and cleaned, and everything made to look like a new pin. But besides duties below, the Stoker is employed very often on deck, where he has to apply his 12 stone or so of matter to the business end of a rope or wire hawser, and aid the Seamen, of whom too many are never supplied!

THE STOKER
(No. 1's).

THE BOY SIGNALLER

is principally employed as a messenger by the Signal Bo'sun or the Yeoman of Signals. He keeps his eyes open in this capacity, and begins to pick up the duties of the higher rating he covets. When he does attain to this exalted degree of " Signalman," his duties are to take in any signals made, either by Semaphore in the day-time, or by Morse at night, keeping a good look out for them all. He reports all ships coming into sight, and all boats which come along-side. He repairs and makes flags, knows what each one means, and is daily employed in carrying out all sorts of signal exercises to keep his hand in. Of course HE also keeps his part of the ship clean, just as the rest of the hands do—and a jolly nice weather-beaten lot these Signalmen are too, always courteous, and ready to do a favour for anyone.

SIGNAL BOY
(No. 2's).

THE ROYAL MARINES

are employed as Sentries, who are placed in various parts of the ship, such as outside the Captain's cabin, Wardroom, or Cells, in the men's Bag Flat, etc. When not doing Sentry-go, they clean ship, hoist boats, and do various other duties such as Postman or Orderly. The Officers' Servants are chosen from the R.M.L.I., who wait at meals as well as keeping their master's cabin and clothes clean and tidy. The "Corporal of the Gangway" is a Marine. His duties, in harbour, are to acquaint the Master-at-Arms when any man, beer or spirits, come into, or leave the ship, etc. Many of the MARINES are employed at Gunnery, as "Gunlayers" or "Sightsetters" or "Gun's Crew."

CORPORAL,
Royal Marine Artillery
(Review Order).

THE
ROYAL MARINE LIGHT INFANTRY

have very similar duties to the Royal Marine Artillery on board. To distinguish them the Artillery are called Blue Marines and the Light Infantry Red Marines. A certain number of Marines are told off every day under a sergeant as the ship's guard. The guard besides furnishing sentries has to fall in on the quarterdeck and salute any Admiral or ship which may be passing. A file of Marines is also landed with the seamen to form a patrol and keep order amongst the liberty men ashore.

PRIVATE,
Royal Marine Light Infantry
(Marching Order).

NAVAL UNIFORMS OF 100 YEARS AGO.

Nelson receiving the Sword of the Wounded Commodore on the
"San Nicolas."

First edition published in 1909 by Gale & Polden Ltd
This edition published in 2020 by the National Maritime Museum
Park Row, Greenwich, London SE10 9NF

ISBN: 978-1-906367-71-8

At the heart of the UNESCO World Heritage Site of Maritime Greenwich are
the four world-class attractions of Royal Museums Greenwich – the National
Maritime Museum, the Royal Observatory, the Queen's House and *Cutty Sark*.

www.rmg.co.uk

Designed by Ocky Murray
Printed and bound in Spain by Grafo

10 9 8 7 6 5 4 3 2 1

Created from an original copy of *Stripes and Types*, first published in 1909
by Gale & Polden Ltd, currently stored in the Caird Library and Archive
(object ID: PBC5565)

The Caird Library and Archive at the National Maritime Museums is the
most extensive maritime reference resource in the world. Available to anyone
interested in maritime history, items can be accessed for free online or in
person, all that is required is to register for a Reader's Ticket. Please contact
library@rmg.co.uk for more information.